I Think You're Grand

A Book for My Grandparent

Written by M.H. Clark

Illustrated by Kelli Flitton

I think it's grand when you spend the day with me. Together, we notice everything...

Like just how big the world is.
And everywhere we go,
it's full of surprises.

I think it's grand how we
can stretch a single afternoon.
There's time for all the very
special things we want to do.

Like adventures and stories
and all kinds of songs.

You sing them first,
then I sing along.

I think it's grand how much we share.

There's some for you...

here's some for me.

That's how it is, with family.

I think it's grand

all the memories we make...

and the magic we find along the way.

Even on the absolutely ordinary days.

BUTTER

I think it's grand how much you know,

and how much you can do.

I love it when you show me how.

Now I can do it too.

I think it's grand
how much we laugh...

How many questions I can ask...
You know the how and what and why...
You teach me new things all the time.

You know what I think, actually?
I think you might know everything.

You know what else I think is grand?
When we're together, hand in hand.

'Cause all my favorite things to do
are much more fun when I'm with you.

And the moments
you might think
are small...
are the ones that
matter most of all.

It's grand to let the day unfold...

Go everywhere we want to go...

It's grand to visit and explore...

I always want five minutes more.

There's so much we can try and do.

I hope that I can see you soon...

Until then, here's a great big hug,

and absolutely all my love.

'Cause more than you might understand...

I think you're just so very grand.

COMPENDIUM.
live inspired

Written by: M.H. Clark
Illustrated by: Kelli Flitton
Edited by: Bailey Vega
Art Directed by: Steve Potter

ISBN: 978-1-957891-57-6

1st printing. Printed in China with soy inks on FSC®-Mix certified paper.

Create meaningful moments with gifts that inspire.

CONNECT WITH US
live-inspired.com | sayhello@compendiuminc.com

@compendiumliveinspired
#compendiumliveinspired